The HALLOWEEN
Activity Book

Buster Books

ILLUSTRATION AND CONCEPT BY PAUL MORAN

WRITTEN AND EDITED BY LAUREN FARNSWORTH

DESIGNED BY BARBARA WARD

First published in Great Britain in 2014 by Buster Books,
an imprint of Michael O'Mara Books Limited, 9 Lion Yard, Tremadoc Road, London SW4 7NQ

W www.busterbooks.co.uk f Buster Children's Books 🐦 @BusterBooks

Additional page materials adapted from shutterstock.com
HAUNTED HOUSE™, House of Terror™ and Spookhouse™ copyright © House Industries

ISBN: 978-1-78055-243-9

2 4 6 8 10 9 7 5 3 1

This book was printed in June 2014 by
Shenzhen Wing King Tong Paper Products Co. Ltd., Shenzhen, Guangdong, China.

Halloween is a frightful night of monsters, ghouls and ghosts. You'll need your wits about you to solve these gruesome games, putrefying puzzles and abominable activities.

Join the grim creatures in these pages and turn frightening into fun.

Squeak!
I am hidden on five pages in this book. Can you find me before the monsters get me?

WEREWOLF IDENTIFIER

Worried your friend might be a werewolf?
Use this checklist on the next full moon to find out.

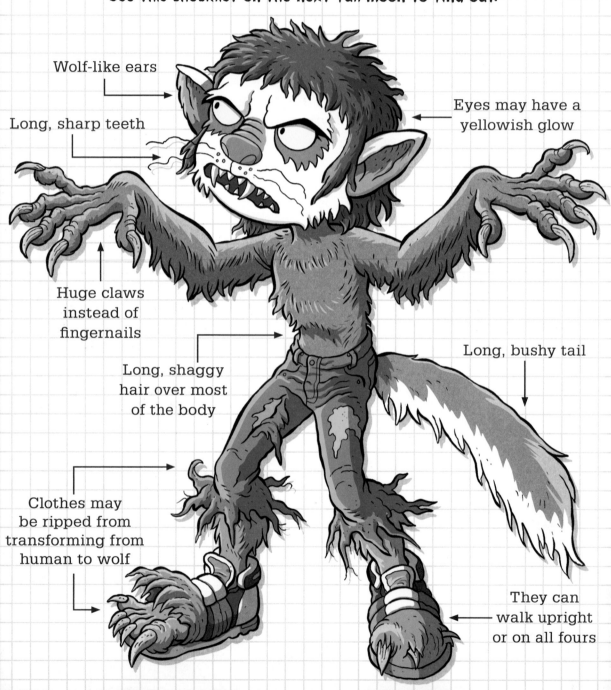

Wolf-like ears

Long, sharp teeth

Eyes may have a
yellowish glow

Huge claws
instead of
fingernails

Long, shaggy
hair over most
of the body

Long, bushy tail

Clothes may
be ripped from
transforming from
human to wolf

They can
walk upright
or on all fours

HE'S 'ARMLESS!

It's not easy being a skeleton – you don't have any skin to keep your bones in. Poor Colin's lost an arm on his way home.

Starting at home, can you help him find which path leads to his lost limb? The answer is at the back of the book.

THE ZOMBIE SHUFFLE

The time may come when you need to blend in with a horde of zombies. Make sure you know the moves.

1. Get into the mindset. Think of your body as something you can't use very well any more.

2. Point your toes slightly inwards. Zombies don't really know which way is forward.

3. Move slowly and, from time to time, stop suddenly mid-walk.

4. Add some zombie injuries. Did you break your leg? Drag it along behind you. Have you dislocated your shoulder? Then hang your arm loosely at your side.

5. Zombie necks don't have strong muscles, so flop your head to one side.

6. Imagine you can smell tasty brains. Reach out randomly to try to grab them. You're not the most co-ordinated grabber though, so make sure your movements are clumsy.

7. Don't forget to moan and groan. Moving around takes its toll — let everyone know how unhappy you are about it.

GHOST DISGUISE

You wouldn't want to look as ghoulish as a ghost in real life, but you can fake it with face paint for a spooky occasion. Here's what to do ...

WHAT YOU WILL NEED:

- White, black and grey face paints
- Sponges.

1. Give your whole face a white base.

2. Blend a small amount of black all around your eyes to make them look sunken.

3. Dab on a small amount of grey paint in patches. Blend these in using a sponge.

4. Rub some black paint over your lips to make them look grey and dry.

5. Wear a white T-shirt to complete your ghostly look.

Now go and show off your fearsome face!

PIECE IT TOGETHER

A hungry werewolf has chewed up this photograph.
Can you tell which pieces below fit into the photo?
Check your answers at the back of the book.

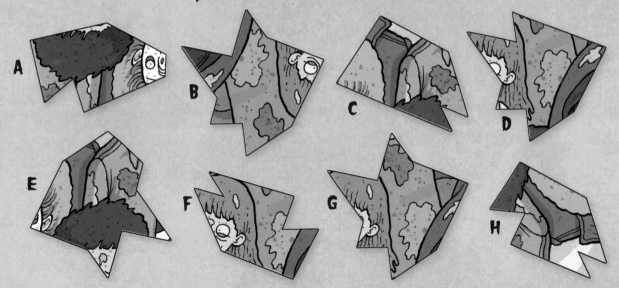

HAVOC AT THE LAB

Some mutants have run riot in the school science lab. Colour in the scene.

THE RULES

If you want to have any chance of surviving a monster attack, you'd better stick hard and fast to this advice.

1. Get fit

The fitter you are, the more chance you have of escaping a monster's clutches. Eat plenty of fruit and vegetables, and do lots of exercise.

2. Arm yourself

A necklace of garlic, a spray bottle of holy water and a sturdy stake are essentials when fighting vampires.

3. Travel in groups

Going out walking alone only gives any ghastly creatures more chance of catching you. Make sure you stick with a group of people — ideally some who can't run as fast as you.

4. Beware a full moon

There's no worse time to be out at night than when a full moon is in the sky. Barricade yourself in a safe place and sit tight until morning.

5. Find shelter

Creatures of the night love dark, mouldy places, so find a bright, uncluttered shelter to hide in. That way, you will always see them coming.

6. Check for bites

Check people for werewolf, zombie or vampire bites before you let them into your shelter — they could be infected!

7. Watch your manners

A witch is likely to leave you in peace unless you anger her. Be sweet and polite or you might find yourself under a nasty spell.

BRAINDEAD

Do you think you're as stupid as a zombie? Try getting all the answers on this quiz **WRONG**. Succeed and you truly are braindead.

1. How long can the brain stay alive without oxygen?

a. 24 hours   **b.** 4–6 minutes

2. What organ weighs twice as much as your brain?

a. Your skin   **b.** Your heart

3. How much does the average human brain weigh?

a. 1.3kg   **b.** 5kg

4. At what age will your brain stop growing?

a. 18 years   **b.** Never

5. How much of your brain is made up of water?

a. 10%   **b.** 75%

6. Which animal has the largest brain?

a. A sperm whale   **b.** An elephant

Check your answers at the back of the book, then find out how dead your brain is below.

1-2 incorrect: Looks like you're too clever to be braindead. Have you considered letting a zombie eat some of your brain?

3-4 incorrect: Not bad. Still room for dumbing down.

5-6 incorrect: Well done! No one would be able to tell the difference between you and a real zombie.

PET CEMETERY

The living dead are walking their pets. Draw some undead pets in the space below.

MONSTER JELLY

Sweet and wobbly – everyone loves jelly! But add a few special ingredients and you can make it fit for Halloween.

WHAT YOU WILL NEED:
- 1 packet of strawberry or raspberry jelly
- 1 jelly mould
- 4 mini brains (walnut halves)
- 6 eyeballs (peeled green grapes)
- A handful of guts (strawberry bootlaces).

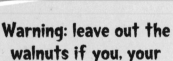

Warning: leave out the walnuts if you, your friends or family have a nut allergy!

1. Make some jelly by following the instructions on the packet. This often involves hot water, so ask an adult to help you.

2. Pour your jelly mixture into the jelly mould.

3. Before putting your jelly into the fridge to set, add four walnut halves.

4. Next, add six peeled green grapes to the mixture.

5. Finally, lower in a few strands of strawberry bootlaces, swirling them around the walnuts and grapes.

6. Put your jelly mixture into the fridge to set, leaving it for as long as the packet suggests.

7. Once the jelly has set, ask an adult to dip the mould in hot water to loosen it and then turn the jelly out on to a plate.

Amazing! You now have jelly fit for a monster. It may look disgusting, but it will taste great.

SPLAT TO SPLAT

Who's lurking outside? Join the gross drips and splats to find out.

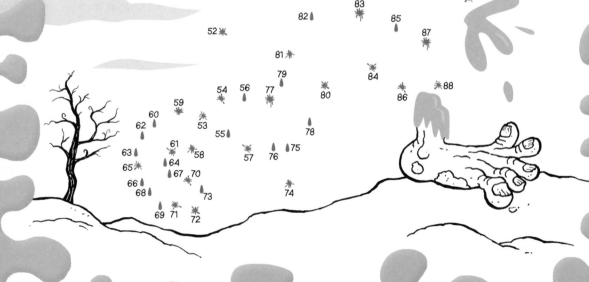

MR FRANKENSTEIN

Many monsters start out as normal humans.
Read the story below and fill in the blanks to create a true tale of terror.

We all made fun of Mr Frankenstein's name. He was such a ....
[great/ happy/ smiley] teacher that it seemed funny for him to have such a
grim name. That was until that frightful day last year.

I knew something was strange from the moment Mr Frankenstein walked into the
classroom. He looked very .... [sick/ grey/ sleepy]. He was
dragging his feet and his skin was .... [peeling/ flaky/
scabby]. I even noticed a long scar running across the middle of his head.

'I'm sorry I'm late,' he said to the class in a ....
[gruff/ slow/ moaning] voice. 'I've not been feeling well. Open your books and
begin the exercise.'

I tried to concentrate, but I couldn't help looking at Mr Frankenstein. He was hunched over his desk, then all of a sudden, he looked up at me with his .... [watery/ bloodshot/ tired] eyes. I kept my head down, but before long, I heard Mr Frankenstein's chair scrape back and his dragging footsteps coming towards me.

Out of the corner of my eye I could see him come to a stop right beside my desk.

'Please see me after class,' he said with a rattling breath.

Before I knew it, it was the end of the lesson. The classroom seemed to empty faster than usual — the room had started to smell of .... [mould/ rotting fish/ wet dog].

'Come here, please,' Mr Frankenstein said quietly. He was clearly finding it difficult to .... [breathe/ speak/ focus].

As I got closer, I could see his .... [skin/ nose/ ears] falling off.

'Sir, are you okay?' I asked.

He turned his head to face me, and I could almost hear his bones .... [crack/ creak/ crunch]. Then, he slowly rolled back the sleeve on his left arm, except ... there wasn't an arm there!

'Would you mind terribly if I borrowed something from you?' he asked.

His breath smelled like .... [boiled cabbage/ cheese/ stinky socks]. Yuk! I instantly knew he wanted to tear my arm off and use it as his own. I knew what had happened to Mr Frankenstein. He'd become a real-life Frankenstein's monster!

'.. [No way/ Get away from me/ Nooooooooooo]!' I screamed and ran out of the door.

Mr Frankenstein followed me down the corridor. He was surprisingly fast for a stitched-together monster. There was only one thing for it — I had to be brave and take him on. But I was feeling so .... [scared/ petrified/ sick].

I swallowed my fear and span around to face Mr Frankenstein. I think he was .... [surprised/ shocked/ stunned], as I was able to quickly grab his right arm and yank HARD. It made a gross .... [squelching/ ripping/ crunching] sound.

I whacked Mr Frankenstein around the head with his own arm. Because he was now completely armless, he lost his balance easily and fell over.

I ran away and didn't look back, and that was the last I saw of Mr Frankenstein. It's strange though, the only person that would have cleaned up a mess like that in the corridor would have been the caretaker, Mr Gormless. And even though I'm sure he's just a sweet old man, sometimes I see him looking at me strangely in the corridor, and there's always that ghastly smell coming from inside his cupboard ...

TIMETABLE OF TERROR

Even monsters have to go to school, though there's not much chance of getting them to learn anything. Fill in this school timetable with all the lessons you think a monster should have.

Subject	Teacher	Lesson
Shapeshifting	Mr Shadow	How to transform into the animal of your choice.
Witchcraft	Ms Bat	How to cook up potions and turn your enemies into pencil sharpeners.
Potions	~~Dr Strange~~ Dr Strange.	Turn your self invisible.

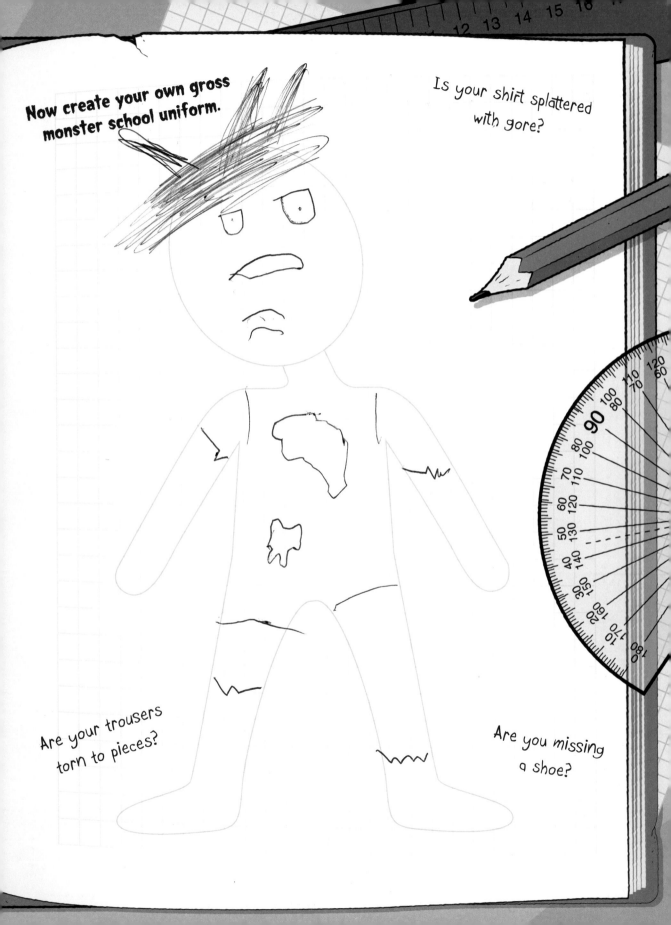

Now create your own gross monster school uniform.

Is your shirt splattered with gore?

Are your trousers torn to pieces?

Are you missing a shoe?

'ORRIBLE ORIGAMI

This scary skull is easy to fold out of paper, and you can even make it talk.

WHAT YOU WILL NEED:
- A large square of paper
- Colouring pens or pencils.

1. Make a cross on your square of paper by folding it corner to corner and then opening it out.

3. Fold the top corner down, as shown by the arrow.

2. Fold it into a kite shape, by bringing the left and right corners to meet in the middle.

4. Fold the long bottom point up so it meets the top of the skull.

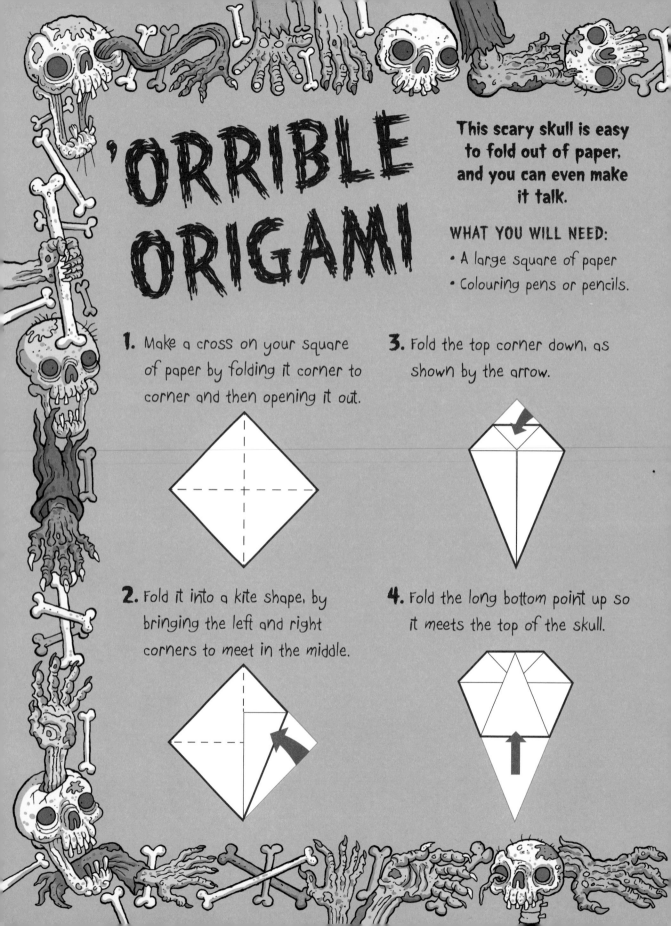

5. Fold the point back down, but leave a little space above your first fold.

6. Turn the paper over.

7. Fold the bottom point up and down five times to make the teeth. Each fold should be the same height.

8. Draw some spooky eyes and a nose on the skull with pens or pencils.

Gently pull the jaw of your skull up and down to make it talk!

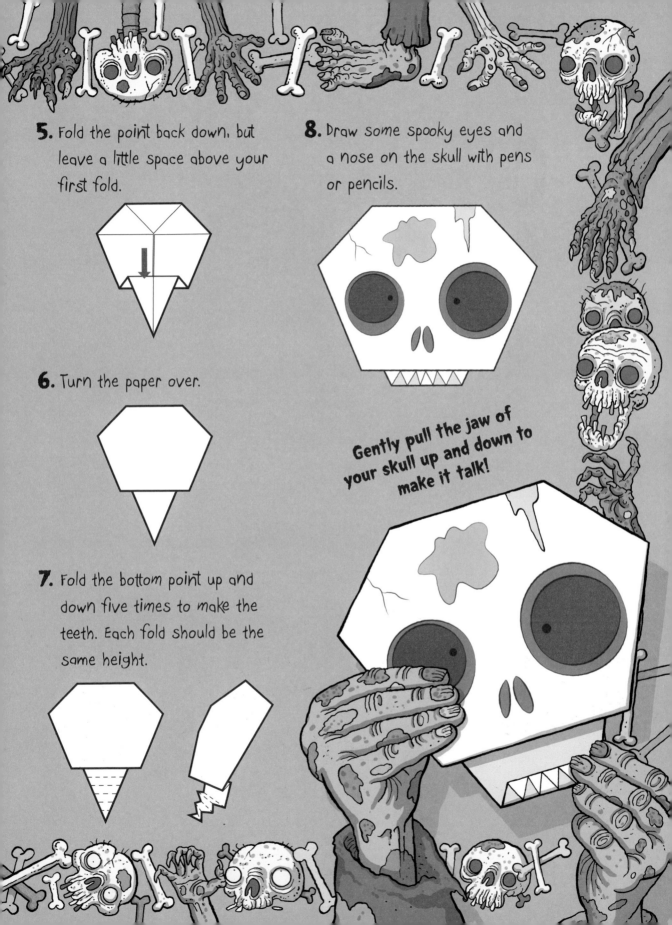

TERRIBLY TRUE OR FOULLY FALSE?

There are seven scary, spooky and sickening stories below. You might wish that they are all made up, but only three of them actually are. Can you guess which ones? The answers are at the back of the book.

Revolting Remedy

In ancient Roman times, eating the brain of a cat was a recommended cure for a chesty cough.

Mice Slice

If you had bad breath in ancient Egypt, one cure was to cut a mouse in two and place one half inside your mouth.

Rest In Peace

When the wife of an English knight called Sir John Price died in the 17th century, he had her body embalmed (preserved). Each night he slept in his bed beside her — even when he married his second wife.

Deathly White

For several centuries in the past, European high-born ladies would cover their faces with white make-up called ceruse. This horrible mixture of white lead and vinegar slowly poisoned them. It caused hair loss, rotting teeth and eventually death.

Doctor Death

In the 18th century, a German doctor called Frederik Franheimer decided to make his very own Frankenstein's monster. He would creep out at night, steal body parts from graves, and take them back to his laboratory. He never got to finish the monster, as he was arrested for grave robbing.

Deadly Ducking

Centuries ago, women accused of witchcraft would be tied to a device called a ducking stool and plunged into water. If they floated they were guilty (and executed), if they drowned they were innocent (but still dead).

A-head Of The Rest

There is a small, rural village in Argentina where it is said that collecting severed heads will bring you great luck.

MUMMY
MUMBLES

Finally – no more trying to guess what mumbling mummies are trying to say. Use this translator to find out what they are saying and also to talk back to them.

What they might say to you	
Mumm-ish	**English**
Meee cuuuur!	I'm cursed!
Oooh tie bandees	My bandages are too tight
Where me go?	How do I get out of this pyramid?
Me Far-oh, yee?	I'm a Pharaoh, don't you know?

What you might say	
English	**Mumm-ish**
Hello	Hee-ohh
What's your name?	Wah ya nah?
Would you mind not chasing me?	Woo mah na chasee?
Get lost!	Geee loz!
What lovely bandages you have	Wah luvvy bandees

MONSTER ME

Imagine what you'd look like as a particularly gruesome Halloween monster, and draw yourself in the frame above.

DEADLY
SPORTS DAY

START

You trip over your own severed arm. Go back 2 spaces.

Your legs are on backwards! Move back 1 space.

It's the eyeball and spoon race, but your arm has fallen off and you've lost your eyeball! Go back 2 spaces to pick it up.

You smell sweet, sticky brains at the finish line – it spurs you on. Skip ahead 3 spaces.

If you think sports day is hard, try doing it as a zombie. Grab counters, dice and a friend, and see who can reach the finish line first.

Your rivals get distracted by something shiny. Skip ahead 1 space.

Your bones get jumbled up in the sack race. Miss a turn while you put them back together.

You fall through a hedge – and find a shortcut.

FINISH

MUTANT MUG SHOTS

Edgar the Eyeless

Give each mutant below a name to describe their gruesome malfunctions. Be as creative as you can. The first one has been done for you.

Don't forget to colour them in!

SCRATCHY SCABS

Here's how to freak out your friends and make some very gross fake scabs.

WHAT YOU WILL NEED:

- A small handful of puffed rice cereal
- A teaspoon
- A small bowl
- 2 teaspoons of golden syrup
- A few drops of red food colouring.

1. Put the cereal in a bowl and crush it into smaller pieces with the back of a teaspoon.

2. Add two teaspoons of syrup.

3. Add a few drops of red food colouring.

4. Mix together well.

5. Spread the mixture on to your skin, and leave for about 10 minutes to dry. The mixture will still be sticky, so make sure your scab doesn't touch anything, especially furniture or clothes.

Now you're ready to scare your friends!

WOULD YOU RATHER ... ?

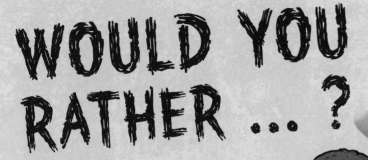

Drool nonstop **OR** have your legs on backwards?

Eat a mouldy sandwich **OR** brain pie?

Have absolutely no teeth **OR** be completely bald?

Be covered in scabs **OR** covered in flies?

Play ping pong with your eyeballs **OR** basketball with your brain?

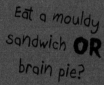

WHAT'S IN THE SKULL?

Doodle what's coming out of this poor Frankenstein's cracked-open head.

BRAINIAC

Think you know everything about Halloween? Put your skills to the test with this brainiac quiz.

1. What is Halloween's full name?
   a. All Hallows' Evening
   b. Hallow We Monsters
   c. Hollow Tree Ghosts

2. What is a popular Halloween phrase?
   a. Trick or trumps
   b. Trick or turnips
   c. Trick or treat

3. What is the original meaning of Halloween?
   a. To eat as much chocolate as possible
   b. To invent new monsters
   c. To remember the dead

4. What might you carve on Halloween?
   a. A turkey
   b. A pumpkin
   c. A pizza

5. What game is popular on Halloween?
   a. An egg hunt
   b. Tree decorating
   c. Apple bobbing

6. On what date do people celebrate Halloween?
   a. 25th December
   b. 1st January
   c. 31st October

Check your answers at the back of the book to get your score and find out if you're a brainiac.

Are you a brainiac?

5-6 correct

Excellent! You're a Halloween expert.

3-4 correct

Not bad, but some improvement needed.

1-2 correct

No good. Back to Monster School for you.

BRAINS
BY NUMBERS

Follow the number key to colour in this brain-tastic circus scene.

1 2 3
4 5 6

WHICH WITCH?

These twin witches are double trouble, causing confusion wherever they go.

Can you spot EIGHT differences between them?

DEAD ENDS

Avoid the obstacles to escape this graveyard maze.

START

END

WHAT'S IN THE BOX?

Want to gross out your friends? Grab some cardboard boxes, cut holes in the tops just big enough for your hand to slip through and fill the insides with these yucky things ...

Make sure to give your boxes gross labels to scare your friends.

EARS

(dried apricots)

EYEBALLS

(peeled grapes)

BRAINS

(a cauliflower smothered in syrup)

MAGGOTS

(a bowl of cold, cooked rice mixed with a little water)

GUTS

(cold, cooked spaghetti)

Oh no, you silly ghoul, you've gone and lost both your arms. Now you have to draw a picture with your foot instead.

See if you can copy the picture on the left by holding a pencil between your toes.

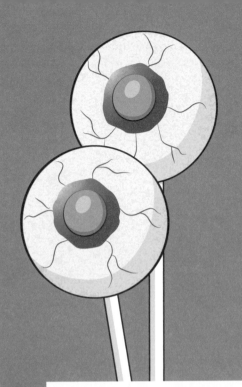

EYEBALL CAKE POPS

Add a dash of fear to a party by making up a batch of these eye-popping treats.

WHAT YOU WILL NEED:

- 1 mixing bowl
- 250g plain sponge cake
- 1 tbsp white icing
- Large block of polystyrene
- Lollipop sticks
- Red food colouring
- Small round sweets (jellies or chocolates)
- A small paint brush.

1. In a mixing bowl, crumble the sponge into fine crumbs.

2. Add the icing, a teaspoon at a time, and mix well into the sponge crumbs until you have a firm mixture that can be rolled into balls.

3. Place two heaped teaspoons of the mixture into your hands and roll into a ball. Repeat until you have about eight cake balls.

4. Place the cake balls into the freezer for about 30 minutes.

5. Using one of your lollipop sticks, poke eight well-spaced holes into one side of the polystyrene. Make sure they are deep enough so the lollipop sticks stand up by themselves.

6. Take the cake balls out of the freezer. Poke a lollipop stick into each cake ball, until it is firmly in place. Hold your cake pops up by placing them into the holes in the block of polystyrene.

7. Push a sweet into each cake pop. These make the irises of the eyeballs.

8. Using a small paint brush and the red food colouring, paint spindly veins over the eyeball cake pops. Try adding a red rim around the sweet for extra-ghoulish eyes.

Yummy!

OFF WITH HIS HEAD

Oh dear. Frank's bolts have come loose and he's lost his head. Can you help him find it?

Frank's head has two ears, hair and no brains visible. The answer is at the back of the book.

HAPPY HEAD HUNTING!

Can you also find eight loose ears?

THE GREAT ESCAPE?

The kids in this story have stumbled across some zombies. Will they escape? You decide ...

Fill in the spaces with your own words and pictures to finish the story.

Oops!

Oh no, everybody at Mr and Mrs Dimwit's barbecue has turned into zombies!

Can you draw Mr Dimwit?

THE MONSTER MAIL

Some monsters might only be myths, but these real-life monster tales from the animal world might keep you up at night.

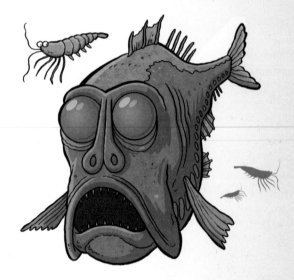

WIGGLING WORMS

Monster mate: zombie

When a certain worm is eaten by a snail, it infects the snail's brain and travels to its antennae. The worm transforms the antennae to look like wiggling maggots and makes the snail crawl in to the open, where birds usually mistake it for a tasty maggot lunch.

FRIGHTENING FISH

Monster mate: demon

The deep-sea hatchetfish is well known for the shape of its body that really does resemble the fine blade of an axe or 'hatchet'. Its terrifying, staring eyes and ghoulish mouth will make you wish you did have an axe to hand if you ever come across one.

LITTLE DEVILS

Monster mate: devil

Screeching, snarling Tasmanian devils are named for their famously feisty bad tempers. They will fly into maniacal rages when threatened, baring their needle-like teeth and launching fierce attacks. They spend their days alone in caves or burrows and emerge to feed when the sun sets, where their spine-chilling screams echo into the night.

SCARY SHARKS

Monster mate: goblin

This unfortunate-looking goblin shark, with a snout just like that of a long goblin's nose, is more funny looking than dangerous. When alive, this shark has strangely pink skin, but when it dies it fades to grey. Living in very deep waters, it doesn't pose a threat to humans. It is, however, a rare and ancient creature, being the only surviving species of a family of sharks over 125 million years old.

THE CURE!

Jimmy the zombie is a bit cleverer than his zombie friends and has invented the zombie cure. Guzzle down this healthy drink whenever you're feeling a bit gormless.

YOU WILL NEED:
- ½ litre of apple juice
- 150g spinach, chopped
- 1 green apple, chopped
- ½ avocado, chopped
- A blender (and an adult to help you).

Combine all the ingredients in a blender ...

Get an adult to help you with the blender.

... then guzzle it down ... wait ... wait.

You're cured!

THE ANSWERS

He's 'Armless!
The correct path is B.

Piece It Together
The correct pieces are B and H.

Braindead (remember: these are the WRONG answers)
1. a   3. b   5. a
2. b   4. b   6. b

Terribly True or Foully False
The false stories are:
Revolting Remedy, Doctor Death
and A-head Of The Rest.

Brainiac
1. a   3. c   5. c
2. c   4. b   6. c

Goodbye Eye
Ringo's eyeball is A.
Sally's eyeball is B.
Marvin's eyeball is C.

Off With His Head
Frank's head is G.